Eine neue Sprache

German Learning for Kids

BABY PROFESSOR

EDUCATION KIDS

Speedy Publishing LLC
40 E. Main St. #1156
Newark, DE 19711
www.speedypublishing.com

ANANAS

Ananas   Ananas

KÄSE

Käse   Käse

Birne Birne

Chamäleon Chamäleon

Review Exercise # 1

Match the German word to its corresponding English translation.

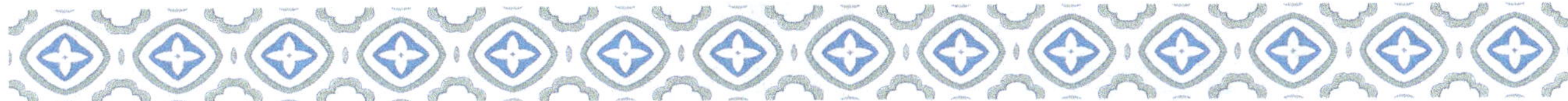

Ananas • • Cheese

Käse • • Pineapple

Birne • • Chameleon

Chamäleon • • Pear

Dinosaurier Dinosaurier

E1

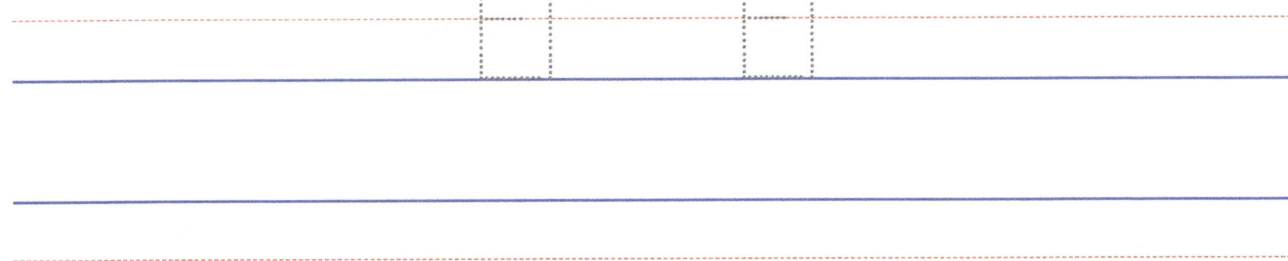

FISCH

Fisch   Fisch

Gans   Gans

Review Exercise # 2

Match the German word to its corresponding English translation.

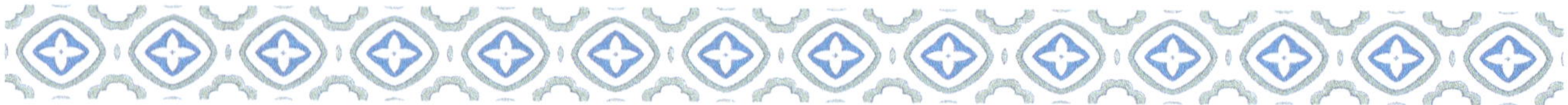

Dinosaurier •   • Goose

El •   • Dinosaur

Fisch •   • Egg

Gans •   • Fish

Hund Hund

Igel   Igel

JOGHURT

Joghurt   Joghurt

KATZE

K

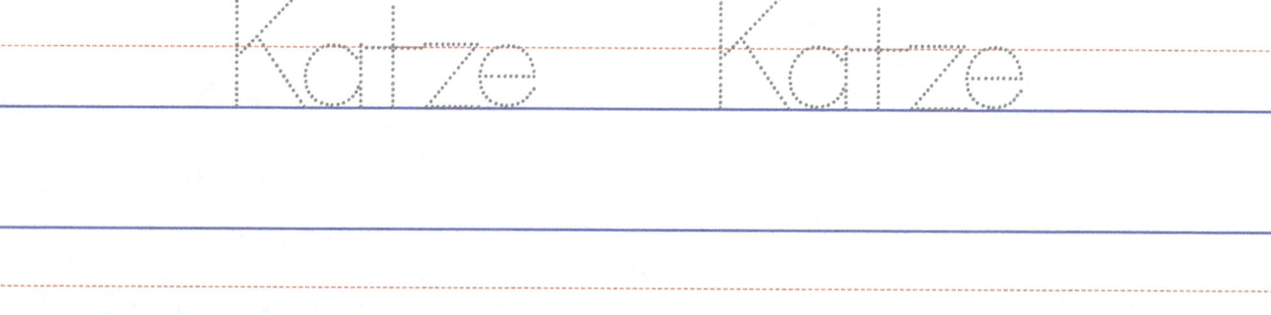

Katze   Katze

Review Exercise # 3

Match the German word to its corresponding English translation.

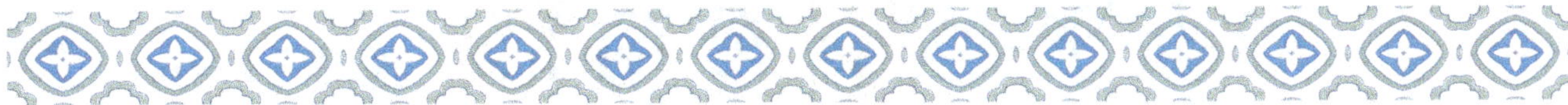

Hund •	• Yogurt
Igel •	• Dog
Joghurt •	• Cat
Katze •	• Hedgehog

LÖWE
L

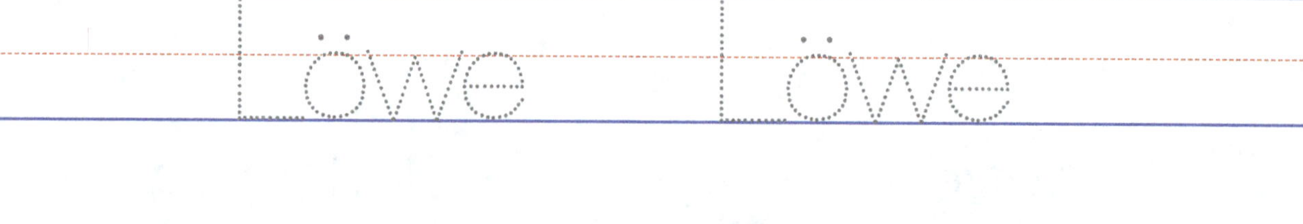

Löwe   Löwe

Maus   Maus

Nadel   Nadel

Orange   Orange

Review Exercise # 4

Match the German word to its corresponding English translation.

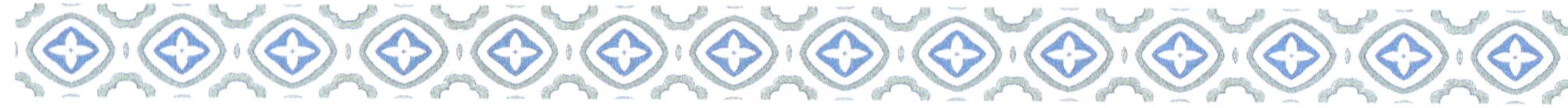

Löwe •		• Mouse
Maus •		• Orange
Nadel •		• Needle
Orange •		• Lion

Öl

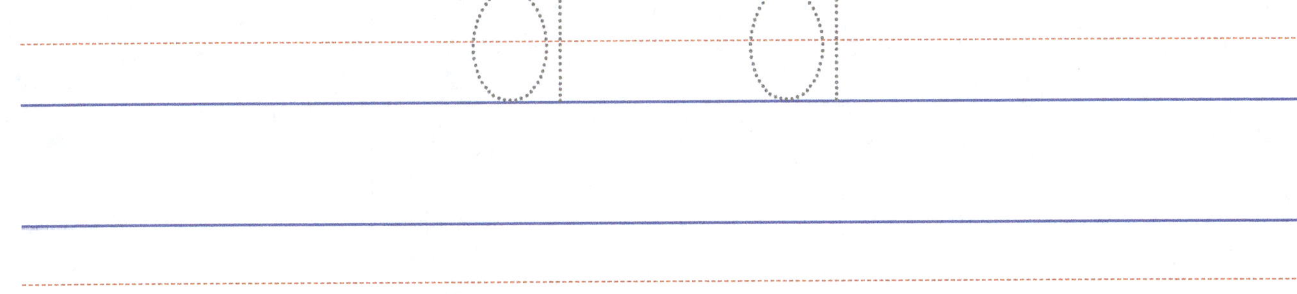

PFERD

Pferd Pferd

QUALLE
Q

Qualle   Qualle

Reiher   Reiher

SCHNECKE

Schnecke   Schnecke

Review Exercise # 5

Match the German word to its corresponding English translation.

Öl •   • Snail

Pferd •   • Olive Oil

Qualle •   • Jellyfish

Reiher •   • Heron

Schnecke •   • Horse

Weißbrot   Weißbrot

TOMATE

Tomate   Tomate

Uhu   Uhu

Tür   Tür

Review Exercise # 6

Match the German word to its corresponding English translation.

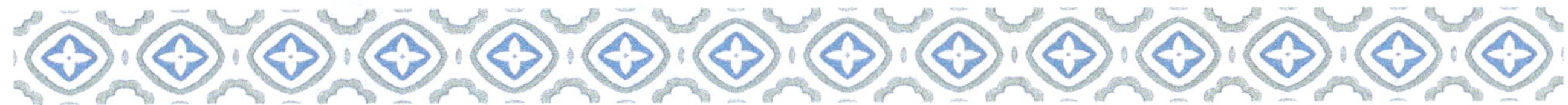

Weißbrot •	• Violet
Tomate •	• Door
Uhu •	• Tomato
Tür •	• Owl

Vogel Vogel

WASSERMELONE

Wassermelone

Xylophon   Xylophon

YETI
Y

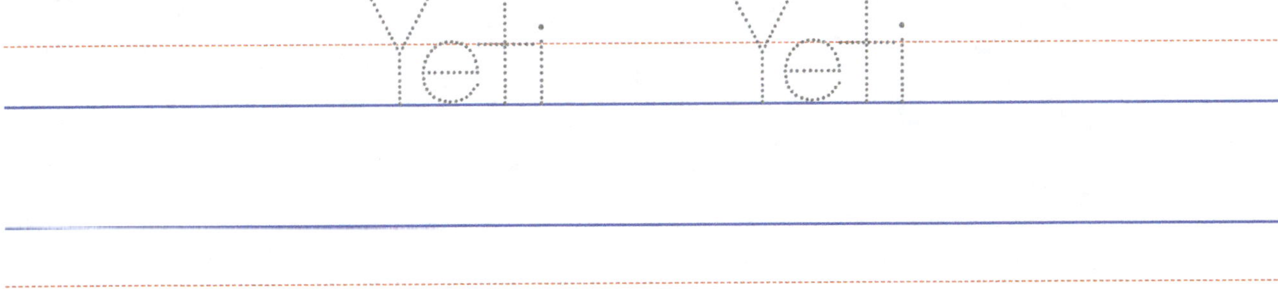

Yeti   Yeti

ZITRONE

Zitrone   Zitrone

Review Exercise # 7

Match the German word to its corresponding English translation.

Vogel •	• Yeti
Wassermelone •	• Xylophone
Xylophon •	• Lemon
Yeti •	• Bird
Zitrone •	• Watermelon

Visit
BABY PROFESSOR
EDUCATION KIDS
www.BabyProfessorBooks.com
to download Free Baby Professor eBooks
and view our catalog of new and exciting
Children's Books

www.ingramcontent.com/pod-product-compliance
Lightning Source LLC
Chambersburg PA
CBHW080817120726
48001CB00009B/2919